TOP LEFT AND CLOCKWISE: SIMPSON DESERT, SOUTHWEST QUEENSLAND; ULURU, NORTHERN TERRITORY; PRECIPITOUS BLUFF, SOUTHWEST TASMANIA;
KATA TJU<u>T</u>A, NORTHERN TERRITORY; THE THREE SISTERS, NEW SOUTH WALES; REMARKABLE ROCKS, KANGAROO ISLAND, SOUTH AUSTRALIA

THE RED CENTRE

The Red Centre of Australia is the driest part of the driest inhabited continent on planet Earth. It was not always so. Until around eight million years ago, Central Australia was humid and covered with rainforest. As the continent became more arid, the forest was replaced by drought-resistant plants.

The animals changed with the climate. Today, the most commonly seen animals of the desert surrounding the ranges are insects, lizards and a few hardy birds. Mammals and seed-eating birds are most common where there is water.

Alice Springs is the base for those who journey through the Red Centre during the cooler part of the year. Red plains dotted with golden triodia "spinifex" stretch to faraway purple ranges, and the Devils Marbles, Chambers Pillar, Kings Canyon and Rainbow Valley are stunning reminders that this most ancient of landscapes holds spectacular rewards for the modern traveller.

TOP LEFT AND CLOCKWISE: THE MUCH-ERODED PETERMANN RANGES; DUNES OF THE SIMPSON DESERT; KINGS CANYON, WATARRKA NATIONAL PARK; CHAMBERS PILLAR (ITIRKAWARA); THE DEVILS MARBLES
OPPOSITE: THE FINKE RIVER RUNS UNDERGROUND IN FINKE RIVER GORGE

ULURU NATIONAL PARK

It is Aboriginal belief that Uluru, that great monolith ten kilometres around, was once a vast sandhill. The deep gullies grooved into its steep sides, the many caves and overhangs were made by the ancestral beings, and each tells a story. The Rock is a sacred place in Aboriginal ritual life and today the 126,000 hectare Uluru National Park is managed jointly by the Aboriginal owners and the Australian Nature Conservation Agency.

Uluru rises 348 metres above the surrounding mulga plain and lies around 450 kilometres southwest of Alice Springs. The cooler months between May and October are the best to explore Uluru and the National Park in which it stands.

TOP LEFT AND CLOCKWISE: ULURU; ULURU AT SUNSET, FRAMED BY DESERT OAKS; ULURU, MAJESTIC MONUMENT; ULURU, PLACE OF LEGEND AND DREAMS

Thirty-two kilometres to the west of Uluṟu is Kata Tjuṯa, once known as the Olgas. Kata Tjuṯa means "place of many heads" and the loftiest of those heads, Mount Olga, is two hundred metres higher than Uluṟu's sandstone crest.

LEFT: AN EAGLE'S-EYE VIEW OF KATA TJUṮA
BELOW: MANY-HEADED KATA TJUṮA

KATA TJUTA

The enormous monoliths which form Kata Tjuta are arranged roughly in a circle, with four of the highest, side by side on the southwestern face, rising straight from the plain. Each of the forty or so "heads" is made from waterworn boulders, some one metre across, cemented together into "puddingstone".

In the canyons between the monoliths, sheltered from the heat of the surrounding plains, are stands of semitropical vegetation.

At present, nearly 400 types of plants, 150 species of birds, 22 mammals and many reptiles and frogs have been recorded from Uluru National Park. Many species are found in the sheltered canyons. Others flourish on the Park's arid plains. If you wish to see the shy animals of the Red Centre, be prepared to wait and watch for them in the magic hours on either side of sunset and sunrise.

THE MACDONNELL RANGES

The red rocks of the MacDonnell Ranges form a backdrop to Alice Springs and run due west from "the Alice" for over 300 kilometres.

Ages ago, colossal pressures wrinkled the Earth's crust, which was heated and hardened into resistant quartzite and less durable shale and slate. Today, from Arltunga to Glen Helen and beyond, the tough quartzite ribs of the old folds remain as the MacDonnell Ranges. The Finke, Hugh and Todd Rivers have gouged openings such as Simpson's Gap and Ormiston Gorge across the mountain remnants.

Visit Alice Springs and be thrilled by the many images of the MacDonnells. There are rock-walls of gold and red-brown, dappled with purple shadow, deep, dark-green pools of cool water, golden clumps of spinifex broken by sentries of twisted blue-grey mulga and, always, shimmering warm-hued stone touching cobalt-blue sky.

ABOVE: A GHOST GUM AND THE MACDONNELL RANGES
BELOW: AERIAL VIEW OF THE MACDONNELL RANGES
OPPOSITE ABOVE AND BELOW: ARID-COUNTRY VEGETATION ; WATER IS A CENTRE FOR WILDLIFE

LITCHFIELD NATIONAL PARK

In Litchfield National Park, two hours' drive south of Darwin, dense rainforest thickets grow in hollows and gorges cut by streams running off the Tabletop Range into the Reynolds River. Tabletop Swamp is the heart-spring which pumps water into catchments running away from the range.

Wangi Falls is one of many attractions in Litchfield. Here, twin falls cascade down a 90 metre drop of jagged quartzite, where ferns spring from a maze of fractures in the rock and echo the verdant greens of the rainforest. The spectacular cascade of Tolmer Falls can be viewed from a platform reached by a walking track.

The road from Batchelor to Wangi provides a magnificent scenic drive, accessing camping spots at Wangi Falls and at beautiful Florence Falls. For the walker, there are the highlights of discovering stands of primeval rainforest and exploring, on the tops, the dramatic formations of the Lost City.

ABOVE: FLORENCE FALLS, LITCHFIELD NATIONAL PARK

KATHERINE GORGE

The sandstones of Katherine Gorge are part of the Arnhem Land Plateau. For millions of years the Katherine River, fed by violent summer monsoon rains, has sliced the plateau into a vast grid of majestic, walled gorges.

Katherine Gorge gives the visitor rare opportunities to participate in adventures by boat, on foot and from the air. Base can be made at Katherine, 29 kilometres away, or from Nitmiluk National Park's excellent camping ground.

The richest experience comes from voyaging by canoe deep into the gorge country just before sunrise. The canoe runs silently across the dark glassy water, as the dawn chorus of unseen birds echoes between the towering walls of rock.

In contrast to the cool gorges are the parched landscapes of the sandstone desert of the plateau. In the right season, the heathy spinifex vegetation carries an incredible variety of wildflowers. It can be hot walking the trails around Katherine Gorge, so make an early start for best wildlife viewing.

ABOVE: KATHERINE GORGE, NITMILUK NATIONAL PARK

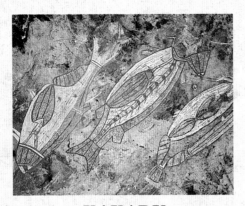

KAKADU
NATIONAL PARK

Kakadu is 250 kilometres east of the modern city of Darwin. The area is dominated by a sandstone plateau which averages 250 to 300 metres in elevation. Countless Wet seasons of monsoonal rains have slashed into its escarpment, and for many hundreds of generations Aboriginal people have sheltered in the caverns and covered the stone with their art.

From January to March, torrential rains fall on the plateau and spectacular waterfalls cascade over the escarpment. Most visitors see Kakadu in the Dry season, between May and September, however there are many rewards for those who visit Kakadu after the rains come.

ABOVE AND CLOCKWISE: ABORIGINAL ROCK ART DEPICTING BARRAMUNDI; STONE COUNTRY, UBIRR; ON THE ESCARPMENT, UBIRR; KAKADU WETLANDS; NOURLANGIE ROCK
OPPOSITE: JIM JIM FALLS

LAWN HILL GORGE

On a hot day, when shimmering mirages break up the hard, deep red sandstone horizon, the track leading west from Gregory Downs or the road going north from Riversleigh across the Gulf Savannah region of northeastern Queensland seems endless. To reach Lawn Hill, turn south-west towards Lawn Hill Park, stop the vehicle and who could imagine that in a hundred steps one would look down on cool, green, lily-covered water? That is the way to discover Lawn Hill Gorge, about 300 kilometres north of Mount Isa and half way between "the Isa" and the Gulf of Carpentaria.

Lawn Hill Creek, fed by countless springs, has cut an impressive gap through the grey limestone. Fig trees hang from the walls of the gorge and narrow gullies are densely packed with Livistona palms and weeping paperbarks.

From December to April, huge volumes of water rush through the gorge to flood the blacksoil plains of the Gulf country. From May to August, Lawn Hill is a warm, sunny paradise.

LEFT: LAWN HILL GORGE
BELOW: CANOEING ON THE GREGORY RIVER

CAPE YORK PENINSULA

Cape York Peninsula, Australia's northernmost promontory, is the size of the State of Victoria. It is still a wild land, a land of mystery, a place for adventure.

On the western side of the peninsula are the Gulf Plains. On the eastern side, the Great Dividing Range rises to over 1,300 metres as it passes from Daintree north to near Cooktown. Here, it is covered with luxurious rainforest, which in places grows right down to the tropical sea. To the north, the Laura Basin drains the Normanby River and its tributaries. North of the Laura Basin are magnificent steamy rainforests, hugging the steep eastern gorges and slopes of the McIlwraith and Iron Ranges. Further north again are the snow-white sand dunes of Cape Flattery, Cape Melville and Shelburne Bay. Then come the vine forests and fan palms of Jardine River National Park and, finally, the place where the Dividing Range dives under Torres Strait.

Cape York is the home of 90 species of native mammals, over half of Australia's 750-odd species of birds, some 50 species of frogs and 158 of reptiles. Fish and insects are still to be tallied.

ABOVE: CAPE YORK, AUSTRALIA'S NORTHERNMOST POINT
BELOW: NEAR SHELBURNE BAY
OPPOSITE: LOOKING TOWARDS CAPE YORK

CAPE TRIBULATION

On the night of 10th June,1770, Captain James Cook and the crew of the *Endeavour* survived their most fearful trial on the Australian coast, when the ship ran aground on a coral reef about 35 kilometres northeast of a point later named Cape Tribulation.

From nearby Port Douglas or Cairns, daytrippers visiting the Cape by boat see pure white beaches, rising to green mountains whose tops may be swathed in mist. After carefully navigating the fringing reef, they reach the shore and make their way onto the crunchy coral rubble and up a beach of delicately tinted sands. Stooping under the scaly grey limbs of massive Calophyllum trees loaded with ferns, epiphytes and orchids, they follow tunnels between the trees into the world of the lowland rainforest. Here, towering figs, propped up by great flying buttresses, are connected by vines to lofty neighbours, under a canopy bathed in rich salmon-coloured flowers alive with shrieking lorikeets. Crystal creeks carve their own green canyons through this paradise of plants and wildlife.

ABOVE: WHERE THE RAINFOREST MEETS THE SEA
BELOW: COOKTOWN ORCHID IS NATIVE TO THE AREA
OPPOSITE: THE BEAUTY OF CAPE TRIBULATION NATIONAL PARK

GREAT BARRIER REEF

The Great Barrier Reef is based on the hard exo-skeletons of uncountable tiny coral polyps, which, with the help of algae, use energy from the sun and take their food from the water. They grow best in shallow, unpolluted, sunlit, constantly moving, well-oxygenated seawater. Like a vast, colourful city, a coral reef develops until it breaks the surface at low tide. Algae growing on the coral is grazed by the reef's herbivores, which become food for more predatory species. The structure becomes a home for fish, molluscs, worms, shells, sponges and other sea-life.

Cyclonic waves, surging tides, currents and the wind attack the reef, scouring away coral rubble and sand, and depositing them as banks and cays. Seeds take foothold and finally gleaming white beach encircles a green oasis of salt-resistant vegetation. A coral island has been born. Animals move into the new living-space. Turtles drag themselves up the beach to lay their eggs. Noddies nest in the bushes and trees, boobies and other birds find sites amidst the coral rubble.

All year round, people from all over the world arrive at the Reef. Some come to dive or fish or sail, others simply dream of paradise in a shining sea. The Reef gives them every chance to realise their dreams.

ABOVE: TOP: BARRIER REEF WATERS; **CENTRE:** BRANCHING CORAL
BELOW: A BARRIER REEF HABITAT
OPPOSITE: LADY MUSGRAVE ISLAND, GREAT BARRIER REEF

THE WHITSUNDAYS

Magnificent centrepiece to Queensland's tropical coast, the Whitsunday Islands are part of the Cumberland Group lying off the shores of Queensland between the towns of Mackay and Bowen. In June, 1770, Captain James Cook recorded, "everywhere good anchorages ... Indeed the whole passage is one continuous safe harbour".

Eighteen thousand years ago, Shute Harbour, which today is the main access for the Whitsundays, was halfway up a rainforest-covered mountainside, separated from the ocean by a broad coastal plain. As an ice age came to its end, immense amounts of water were released into the sea. By 6,000 years ago, 100 metres of water had drowned the coastal plain and the valleys and in place of the mountains there were forest-topped islands.

Today, these islands are fringed with brilliant bays and beautiful estuaries. They harbour secret coves and rich mangrove flats and many are surrounded by coral reef. There are 80 islands, seven of them harbouring resorts. Most of the islands are national parks, easily accessible by water taxi, ferry, cruise boat or helicopter from Shute Harbour, Airlie Beach or Hamilton Island.

ABOVE LEFT TO RIGHT: HILL INLET; NARA INLET; WHITSUNDAY ISLAND
BELOW: PENTECOST ISLAND RISES ABRUPTLY FROM THE SEA
OPPOSITE: GLORIOUS WHITEHAVEN BEACH ON WHITSUNDAY ISLAND

THE GREAT SANDY REGION

The Great Sandy Region stretches along the coast of southern Queensland. For countless years, sand swept by rivers from the Great Dividing Range into the Pacific Ocean was carried northwards. It was deposited to form the sandmasses which today are Fraser Island, Cooloola and the islands of Moreton Bay.

More than 400,000 years ago, the wind commenced the work of shaping this coast of sand. Today, Fraser Island, on the edge of the continental shelf, is the greatest body of sand in the world, 123 kilometres from north to south and averaging 14 kilometres across. Its sand dunes reach a height of 240 metres and it was the first place to be listed on the Register of the National Estate, in 1976. Abundant rain falls on Fraser Island and it contains over 40 dune lakes and many beautiful freshwater creeks.

Cooloola is an area bounded by the Pacific, Tin Can Bay and the Noosa River and lies 150 kilometres north of Brisbane. Its Aboriginal name echoes the sound made by the sea-breeze passing through the coastal cypress pines. Here are dune lakes, lily-covered swamps, aged paperbark trees, heathlands which burst into flower in late winter and early spring, and the famous cliffs of coloured sand.

The Great Sandy Region was recognised as a World Heritage area in 1974. Fraser Island is the world's largest sand island and a place of enormous significance on the grounds of its fauna, flora, Aboriginal history and the fact that it is an encyclopaedia of sand dune types.

ABOVE LEFT TO RIGHT: BLUE LAKE, FRASER ISLAND; COLOURED SANDS, COOLOOLA; CHAMPAGNE POOLS, FRASER ISLAND
BELOW: ONE OF FRASER ISLAND'S MAGNIFICENT BEACHES
OPPOSITE: WOONGOOLBYER CREEK, FRASER ISLAND

THOSE ENDLESS PLAINS

The surface of Australia has been abraded so that mighty mountains are shadows of their former grandeur and hills have been reduced to plains.

West of the Great Dividing Range, from central Queensland south to southern New South Wales, are wide, flat plains. Much of this country is covered with a network of dry creek channels. Grasses and drought-tolerant shrubs survive the dry periods and when rain falls, sometimes hundreds of kilometres away, the creeks fill and overflow their banks and bring new life to the plainlands.

Further west, the grassy plains become arid country, flooded at infrequent intervals by water which drains into salt lakes then evaporates.

The gibber plains which form the stony deserts of the centre are pleasant places for a brief winter visit. In summer, they are ovens where heat-hazes dance forever over shining, shimmering stones.

ABOVE: THE ENDLESS PLAINS OF WESTERN QUEENSLAND
OPPOSITE ABOVE: GIBBERS ON STURT'S STONY DESERT
OPPOSITE BELOW: A TREE MAY GROW IN THE DESERT WHERE IT TAPS
AN UNDERGROUND WATER SOURCE

CARNARVON GORGE

The Maranoa, Barcoo, Bulloo, Warrego and Dawson rivers rise in the Carnarvon Ranges, 485 kilometres northwest of Brisbane. Carnarvon has cliffs and plateaus of immaculate white Precipice Sandstone laid down about 150 million years ago. They are surrounded by rich black soil eroded from a capping of basalt which once covered the older sandstones. Leichhardt's party sighted the area in 1844 and reported that they saw "... a carpet of evergreens for six or seven miles and then the high ranges rose up and formed a beautiful backdrop to the most pleasing natural picture we have seen". Leichhardt called the gorge "Ruined Castle Valley".

Carnarvon National Park includes about 250,000 hectares of the Consuelo Tableland. The Gorge is a ravine over 30 kilometres in length and 50 to 400 metres wide. Spring-fed Carnarvon Creek runs beneath cliffs of white sandstone, on the surface of which are to be seen Aboriginal artworks. Lush vegetation provides a haven for wildlife throughout the ranges.

ABOVE: TOP LEFT AND CLOCKWISE: ABORIGINAL STENCILS; GREY KANGAROO AND JOEY; ABORIGINAL ENGRAVING; SHEER GORGE WALLS TOWER OVER COOL WATER; LAUGHING KOOKABURRAS; EXPLORING CARNARVON CREEK
BELOW: CARNARVON GORGE, A PLACE OF TIMELESS BEAUTY
OPPOSITE: TOP LEFT AND CLOCKWISE: TREEFERNS IN CARNARVON GORGE; BRUSHTAIL POSSUM WITH CYCAD FRUIT; THE WALLS OF THE GORGE RISE TO 200 METRES; PRETTY-FACE WALLABY

LAMINGTON NATIONAL PARK

Twenty million years ago, the Mount Warning shield volcano was a grey hump of a mountain 75 kilometres across, its rainforest-covered sides slashed by gorges and gullies. From time to time, streams of incandescent lava cut smoking paths down through the green forest.

Today, one can drive just over 100 kilometres south from the city of Brisbane to Binna Burra and walk the rainforest-enclosed Border Track to Wagawn Lookout. South, beyond the cliffs of the border ranges, lies the fertile valley carved by the Tweed River from the volcanic rocks surrounding the heart of the old volcano. Mount Warning is a spine 1156 metres high, the remains of a core of dense rock which finally blocked the volcano's vent.

The Border Track from Mount Hobwee to O'Reilly's Guest House follows the spectacular rim of the McPherson Range, which is part of that ancient volcano. There is beauty here at every turn of the track, which zig-zags through strangling figs, brush box, huge buttressed booyongs, walking stick palms dripping with vermilion berries and groves of feathery piccabeen palms.

ABOVE: RAINFOREST, LAMINGTON NATIONAL PARK
OPPOSITE: CHALAHN FALLS, LAMINGTON NATIONAL PARK

THE WARRUMBUNGLES

Australia has had many fiery volcanic episodes in its long history. The Warrumbungle Mountains, Glasshouse Mountains, Mount Warning and Nandewar Mountains are the remains of ancient volcanoes, their contours blurred by time and erosion. About five hours' drive west of Sydney, the town of Coonabarabran, hub of a prosperous agricultural area, provides a base for visits to the Warrumbungle National Park.

The landscape here is a chaos of bold mountains, rugged ridges and sky-piercing spires. It is said that the name "Warrumbungle" is an echo of the thunder of summer storms reverberating about the peaks.

Climbers who reach the Grand High Tops ridge can see the hundred-metre-high Breadknife, where molten rock poured into a split and hardened before being exposed by thirteen million years of erosion. To the right, is four hundred-metre-high Belougery Spire and behind it is Crater Bluff, the vast, split core of another, larger volcano.

The walker can follow tracks which link many of the major mountains, each leading to dramatic lookouts from which can be viewed hundreds of kilometres of western plains and slopes.

ABOVE: THE WARRUMBUNGLES ARE MAGNETS FOR THE BUSHWALKER AND NATURE-LOVER
OPPOSITE: THE BREADKNIFE, A SPECTACULAR MONUMENT IN THE WARRUMBUNGLES

THE BLUE MOUNTAINS

The Blue Mountains lie across Sydney's western horizon, sometimes mauve, sometimes palest lilac, sometimes cobalt, but always beckoning. There is an adventure here for everyone. Govetts Leap, the Three Sisters, Echo Point, the Grand Canyon, Centennial Glen, Blackheath Glen and Wentworth Falls - these are names which mean spectacular scenery and challenges and rewards for the bushwalker and the nature-lover.

Lookouts perched on the valley rims near the lovely town of Katoomba offer magnificent views of majestic sandstone cliffs, fissured by the Grose and Kedumba Rivers. Bridal Veil Falls, Diamond Falls and other cascades plummet hundreds of metres into the blue depths of forested valleys, which in winter echo to the glorious melodies of the Superb Lyrebird.

And the blue of the Blue Mountains? One theory is that eucalyptus oils vaporising from the forest trees lend the ranges their entrancing colour.

ABOVE LEFT TO RIGHT: CLIFFS BROOD OVER THE JAMISON VALLEY;
KATOOMBA SCENIC SKYWAY; VICTORIA FALLS
BELOW LEFT TO RIGHT: MORNING MIST; MOUNTAIN DEVIL, FLORAL SYMBOL
OF THE BLUE MOUNTAINS; RAMPARTS OF SANDSTONE
OPPOSITE: THE THREE SISTERS SYMBOLISE THE BLUE M0UNTAINS

JERVIS BAY

One hundred and eighty kilometres south of Sydney, the entrance to Jervis Bay is guarded by sandy Beecroft Peninsula and Cape St George, whose seaward faces are cliffs of iron-stained sandstones.

From Point Perpendicular on Beecroft, with its crowning lighthouse, the viewer looks across kilometres of heathland to the industrial city of Wollongong and beyond. To the west, the larkspur-blue ranges of Morton National Park run down to Pigeon House Mountain. Across the Bay are the southern peninsula and the wild coast.

ABOVE RIGHT: POINT PERPENDICULAR
RIGHT: MURRAYS BEACH
BELOW: BOWEN ISLAND
OPPOSITE: GREEN PATCH BEACH

Jervis Bay offers lakes, dunes, swamps and sandstone plateaus, coastal bays and beautiful inlets such as Murrays Beach and Green Patch Beach.

THE AUSTRALIAN ALPS

In southeastern Australia, the Great Dividing Range makes a huge zigzag where the land has been weakened by a series of long parallel fractures in the Earth. The Murrumbidgee, Murray and Snowy Rivers have etched their headwaters into these great faults. Much of this country is a high plateau, its northern end landmarked by Mount Kosciusko. Southwards, the high country crosses the Victorian border, swinging west to Mount Feathertop, then north again to Mount Bogong. The rounded granite tops of the Main Range rise to Mount Kosciusko's summit, 2,228 metres above sea-level.

In winter, the mountain slopes are covered by virgin drifts of snow, studded with the glistening trunks of snow gums. In summer, the alpine meadows are glorious with white and golden snow daisies, patches of pink triggerplants and yellow buttercups, nestling among the grey granite tors.

ABOVE: THE MOUNTAIN PYGMY-POSSUM WINTERS IN TUNNELS UNDER THE SNOW
BELOW LEFT TO RIGHT: THE HIGH COUNTRY IN SPRINGTIME; DAWN IN THE AUSTRALIAN ALPS; A WINTER WONDERLAND
OPPOSITE: A WINTERBOUND SNOW GUM

THE GRAMPIANS

The Grampians, which terminate Australia's Great Dividing Range, are only four hours' drive from Mildura, two from Warrnambool and three from Melbourne. Using Halls Gap as base, visitors have unrivalled opportunities for driving and walking amongst grand scenery.

The summits of Mount Abrupt and Mount Victory, of the Jaws of Death, of Sundial and D'Alton Peaks present vistas with few equals anywhere else in Australia. The Wonderland area is remarkable for the fantastic features erosion has wrought from its grey, lichen-encrusted sandstone. Local mecca for adventurers is Mount Arapiles, isolated on the western sandplains, 35 kilometres from Horsham.

ABOVE: A SANDSTONE FANTASY IN NATURE'S WONDERLAND
BELOW: THE GRAMPIANS TERMINATE THE GREAT DIVIDING RANGE
OPPOSITE: MCKENZIE FALLS, A MAGNIFICENT FEATURE OF THE GRAMPIANS

PORT CAMPBELL NATIONAL PARK

The coast of soft, shelly limestone cliffs extending from Port Fairy to Cape Otway is under constant attack by the Southern Ocean. In wild winter weather, lines of waves foam over reefs and the stumps of old rocky headlands and smash into the cliffs or rush up the narrow beaches. That flurry of foam, carrying sand and pieces of broken rock, grinds into structural weaknesses, sometimes penetrating 100 metres into the base of the cliff. Later, during a storm, a huge wave roars in, trapping air before it, a weak place in the roof of the tunnel gives way and a blowhole is formed. Finally, the tunnel collapses to form a narrow bay.

The Port Campbell coastline is a maze of these bays, coves, grottoes, tunnels, isolated sea stacks and stone bridges (which, like the recently-fallen London Bridge, can collapse dramatically). It is an area of unbelievable beauty and grandeur.

The Port Campbell coastline has a dramatic name - "The Shipwreck Coast". It is a part of Australia full of history as well as beauty.

ABOVE LEFT: THE GREAT OCEAN ROAD ACCESSES A SPECTACULAR COASTLINE
ABOVE RIGHT: THE TWELVE APOSTLES ARE STACKS CUT OFF FROM THE MAINLAND
BELOW LEFT AND RIGHT: LONDON BRIDGE BEFORE IT FELL; LONDON BRIDGE AFTER THE FALL
OPPOSITE: THE TWELVE APOSTLES ARE SPECTACULAR LANDMARKS ON "THE SHIPWRECK COAST"

THE OTWAY RANGES

The Otway Ranges extend from Cape Otway to Anglesea, dropping to Bass Strait on their southern side. Their magnificent forests were logged for many years, but are now protected in State and national parks. A walk into this forest from the Great Ocean Road takes one into a world of ancient myrtle beech trees and a wealth of ferns, brooks and shimmering waterfalls. Such forest once covered much of Australia, but is now found only here, in Gippsland and in Tasmania.

Rainforest green gives way to eucalypt greygreens up the drier slopes of the Otways. Here are manna gums, with their streamers of loose bark, leathery mountain grey gums, rough-barked messmates and pale-trunked southern blue gums.

ABOVE LEFT AND RIGHT: ERSKINE FALLS; BEAUCHAMP FALLS
BELOW: MELBA GULLY IN THE OTWAY RANGES
OPPOSITE: HOPETOUN FALLS

TASMANIAN WILDERNESS

The Island State contains a wealth of national parks, which offer many of Australia's most magnificent landscapes. Wild and remote, southwestern Tasmania contains especially spectacular country. In Southwest National Park, soaring mountain ranges, some peaks exceeding one thousand metres in height, sweep in vast saw-toothed curves. Almost without foothills, their sheared and twisted white quartzite raking the sky, the Frankland and Arthur Ranges conceal hanging lakes nestling beneath curving cliffs, the result of long-ago glaciation.

Other glaciated landforms occur in the majestic Cradle Mountain-Lake St Clair National Park, where jagged peaks rise above icy lakes and walkers who venture the famous Overland Track have access to scenes of primeval beauty.

Between the two areas, and completing a band of high-country wilderness, is the superb Franklin-Lower Gordon Wild Rivers National Park.

ABOVE: CRADLE MOUNTAIN-LAKE ST CLAIR NATIONAL PARK
BELOW: DOVE LAKE, CRADLE MOUNTAIN-LAKE ST CLAIR NATIONAL PARK, IN NORTHWEST TASMANIA
OPPOSITE: ARTHUR RANGES, SOUTHWEST NATIONAL PARK

THE FLINDERS RANGES

The picturesque Flinders Ranges stretch over a distance of 430 kilometres, from Marree south to Crystal Brook. On their southern end is Mount Remarkable, named by Matthew Flinders on his circumnavigation of the continent.

The spirit of the ranges is in the river red gums, the chains of craggy peaks and the free flight of Wedge-tailed Eagles soaring high above ridges and valleys. This is a turbulent landscape. The ranges climb above one thousand metres; they dip into deep basins called pounds; they have been carved into rugged gorges by streams and floodwaters.

In the Flinders Ranges, there is a magic half-hour at dawn, when river red gums are silhouetted against the silver sky and dark pools in the creekbed reflect the last rays of starlight, before the rising sun shows Yellow-footed Rock Wallabies feeding on stony hillslopes.

LEFT: RIVER RED GUM, FLINDERS RANGES
ABOVE: RUGGED RANGES RISE FROM GOLDEN PLAINS
BELOW: STURT'S DESERT PEA IS THE FLORAL EMBLEM OF SOUTH AUSTRALIA

KANGAROO ISLAND

In 1802, while circumnavigating Australia, Matthew Flinders and his crew landed on an island 15 kilometres off the southern coast of the continent. Here they found incredibly tame kangaroos, 31 of which they ate.

Kangaroo Island measures about 160 by 60 kilometres. Originally part of the Mount Lofty Range, it was joined to the mainland until about 6,000 years ago. Only 110 kilometres from Adelaide, the island is easily reached by ferry. Its coastal landscapes are varied. There are broad beaches, like that at Seal Bay, which is home to a colony of about 500 Australian Sea-lions. Towering granite cliffs rise from the sea at Cape Willoughby and sitting on the top of a smooth granite dome by Cape du Couedic are the Remarkable Rocks, giant, colourful boulders which have been sculpted by weathering into wonderful forms. Flinders Chase National Park, with its wild rivers and forests, retains what is most natural on the island and is famous for its wildlife.

ABOVE LEFT TO RIGHT: KANGAROO ISLAND SCENES
BELOW: ADMIRALS ARCH
OPPOSITE: REMARKABLE ROCKS

SOUTH COAST OF WESTERN AUSTRALIA

Along the south coast of Western Australia, from Cape Leeuwin to Cape Arid, immaculate white beaches separate headlands of shining silver-grey granite. Offshore, the waves of the Southern Ocean break and retreat from the rounded flanks of continental islands.

All along this southern coast, glorious beaches blend into coastal sandplains and tall trees border placid rivers flowing to the sea in sheltered inlets. Fitzgerald River, Cape Arid and Two Peoples Bay-Mount Manypeaks National Parks offer wild coasts and calm seashores. Inland are heathlands which, in springtime, are bright with multi-coloured wildflowers and sweet-voiced birds.

LEFT: COASTAL SCENE, CAPE ARID NATIONAL PARK
BELOW: AT TWO PEOPLES BAY

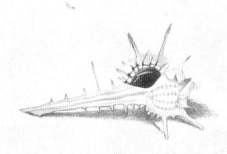

THE NAMBUNG DESERT

The Nambung Desert is part of a long stretch of coastal plain, which is situated about 250 kilometres north of Perth. Until about 35,000 years ago, the area was under the sea and the warm, shallow waters teemed with life. Masses of shells and sand were beached, then swept by the wind into dunes. As the sea receded, the dunes were colonised by coastal trees and shrubs. Centuries of rain seeping through the shelly sand dissolved out lime, which settled around the roots of the plants and solidified as cement. Then came fire, and the area became an inferno. Afterwards, the land lay barren and the wind scoured the exposed sand away from stony pillars which once were roots. Eventually, the Pinnacles stood as pillars of limestone of myriad sizes in Nambung's painted desert.

Seventeenth-century Dutch navigators, who saw these "tombstones of dead plants" after running before the westerly winds across the wild Indian Ocean, thought that they were looking upon the ruins of a city.

August to October, after a wet winter, is the time to visit the Nambung National Park and to wander the flowering heath, amongst the carousing honeyeaters.

ABOVE: THE PINNACLES STAND IN NAMBUNG NATIONAL PARK
OPPOSITE: DUTCH SAILORS THOUGHT THESE PILLARS WERE THE TOWERS OF A RUINED CITY

SHARK BAY

Steep Point, Shark Bay, Western Australia, is as far west as one can go on the Australian mainland. Almost touching the coast is Dirk Hartog Island, where, in 1616, the captain of the Dutch vessel *Eendracht* set an inscribed pewter dish.

Shark Bay, just over 800 kilometres north of Perth, is really two bays, divided by the low Peron Peninsula. At Hamelin Pool, hectares of slow-growing stromatolites, whose ancestors were amongst the planet's earliest lifeforms, stand in the warm, salty water. The most popular experience at Shark Bay is to wade knee-deep at Monkey Mia and stand amongst the sleek wild Bottlenosed Dolphins as they accept offerings of fish and meet their human admirers.

On beds of seagrass in the bay graze about one thousand Dugong, gentle, rare creatures which live in relative peace in these protected waters.

ABOVE TOP: CAPE PERON, SHARK BAY
ABOVE: STROMATOLITES IN HAMELIN POOL, SHARK BAY
OPPOSITE: ZUYTDORP CLIFFS

THE PILBARA

Subject to violent summer cyclones and searingly hot from October to February, in winter the isolated Pilbara region of north-west Western Australia has superbly warm days and cold nights. It has become the destination of motor campers, who arrive each July and August, then follow the spectacular explosion of West Australian wildflowers, which finishes two and one-half thousand kilometres away, beyond Albany, in December. The Pilbara area contains five large national parks, including Hamersley National Park, with its spinifex-covered plateaus slashed with vivid red-and-black gorges. The springs which feed the lily-covered ponds of the Fortescue River at Millstream are oases in a sunbaked world.

The red rocks of the region were laid down two billion years ago. Today, the iron ore which permeates the area is being extracted on a colossal scale.

The coast west of the Pilbara offers wilderness beaches and headlands of red sandstone and limestone swept by clear Indian Ocean waters. Visitors can enjoy the wonderful marine life which exists around the reefs of Ningaloo Marine Park, at Exmouth.

ABOVE: THE PILBARA, AN AREA OF DRAMATIC BEAUTY
OPPOSITE: THE FAMED "MARBLE BAR", WHICH GIVES A NEARBY
PILBARA TOWN ITS NAME, IS MADE OF JASPER

THE KIMBERLEY

Highway One, which takes travellers around Australia, provides access to much of the Kimberley. In the north, five rivers meet at Wyndham, before flowing into Cambridge Gulf. Some distance up the Ord River is the huge dam called Lake Argyle, nine times the size of Sydney Harbour. At the head of the Ord are the wonderful Bungle Bungles, a stupefying maze of haystack-shaped mountains reserved as Purnululu National Park.

For 400 kilometres, the highway slides between ranges which are replaced beyond Halls Creek by low, heat-hazed plateaus. These finally give way to the Fitzroy River flood plains, where portly grey boab trees stand amidst termite mounds. The grey, broken limestone of this area was once a coral barrier reef, which grew long ago beneath a warm salty sea. It is a wonderful experience to explore the 14 kilometres of the Fitzroy River as it flows through Geikie Gorge, with its 16 metre walls. Windjana Gorge displays even more spectacular limestone formations. On the northwest Kimberley coast is the Prince Regent River area, today one of the planet's last true wild places.

ABOVE LEFT TO RIGHT: "THE GREAT WALL OF CHINA", NEAR HALLS CREEK; THE BUNGLE BUNGLES ;
KIMBERLEY COAST IN THE PRINCE REGENT NATIONAL PARK
BELOW LEFT TO RIGHT: THE FITZROY RIVER CUTS THROUGH THE KING LEOPOLD RANGE;
LENNARD RIVER FALLS; PRINCE REGENT NATIONAL PARK
OPPOSITE: THE FITZROY RIVER FLOWS THROUGH GEIKE GORGE

THE ABORIGINAL PEOPLE AND THE LANDSCAPE

The relationship between the Aboriginal people and the land is traditionally not one of "ownership", but rather of "oneness", of being one entity. Groups of Aboriginal people have long been responsible for maintaining the dreaming sites with which their Ancestors were associated, and for passing on the stories about them. It has been customary to enact ceremonies at these traditional sites.

Across Australia, there are rocks with Aboriginal engravings, stencils and paintings upon them. These include some of the oldest works of art known anywhere in the world, some of which have been maintained to the present era, in a tradition which has extended for tens of thousands of years in some areas. The significance and meaning of these works can be comprehended properly only by the Aboriginal people responsible for them. People from other cultures are free to wonder at the record they provide of ages-old interaction between groups of people and the land which nurtured them, physically and spiritually.

LEFT ABOVE AND BELOW: HAND STENCILS FROM CENTRAL QUEENSLAND
CENTRE ABOVE AND BELOW: PAINTINGS FROM TROPICAL NORTHERN TERRITORY
RIGHT ABOVE AND BELOW: ROCK ENGRAVINGS FROM CENTRAL AUSTRALIA
OPPOSITE: LANDFORMS SUCH AS KATA TJUTA ARE PART OF THE BEING
OF THE ABORIGINAL PEOPLE OF THE AREA

TORRES STRAIT

C York

Bathurst Island   Melville Island

DARWIN   Arnhem Land

TIMOR SEA

Cape York Pen

GULF OF CARPENTARIA

Wyndham
Kimberley Division
Derby
Broome
Halls Creek

Katherine

Borroloola

Burketown

NORTHERN TERRITORY

CORAL SEA

Great Barrier Reef

Cooktown

Cairns

Great Dividing Range

Townsville

QUEENSLAND

INDIAN OCEAN

Port Hedland
Marble Bar
Pilbara
North West Cape
Exmouth
Tropic of Capricorn

Great Sandy Desert

Tennant Creek

Mount Isa

Winton

Longreach   Rockhampton   Tropic of Capricorn

WESTERN AUSTRALIA

MacDonnell Ranges   Alice Springs

Simpson Desert   Birdsville

Charleville

Bundaberg
Fraser Is
Sunshine C

SHARK BAY
Carnarvon
Dirk Hartog Is

Great Victoria Desert

SOUTH AUSTRALIA

BRISBANE
Toowoomba   Gold Coast
C Byron

Bourke
Cobar
Broken Hill

Geraldton

Kalgoorlie
Goldfields

Port Augusta
Port Pirie
Murray River
Wentworth

NEW SOUTH WALES

PACIFIC OCEAN

INDIAN OCEAN
Rottnest Is   PERTH
Fremantle
Bunbury
C Naturaliste
C Leeuwin   Albany

Esperance   C Arid

GREAT AUSTRALIAN BIGHT

EYRE PEN
Port Lincoln
Victor Harbor
Kangaroo Is

ADELAIDE
Swan Hill
Echuca

Terrigal

Albury
A.C.T.

Great Dividing Range

SYDNEY
CANBERRA

SOUTHERN OCEAN

VICTORIA
Ballarat
Geelong   MELBOURNE
Warrnambool

TASMAN SEA

BASS STRAIT

Burnie   Launceston
TASMANIA   Richmond

South West Cape   HOBART